You're
DRIVI
CRAZY!

101 Dangerous, Inappropriate, Discourteous, Illegal, and Just Plain Stupid Driving Habits!

John Reinhardt

You're Driving Me Crazy!

USA edition

ISBN: 979-8-9876310-0-3 (Paperback)
ISBN: 979-89876310-1-0 (eBook)

For information contact:

John Reinhardt
13216 Legends Trail
Dade City, FL 33525
802-236-4147
www.YoureDrivingMeCrazy.com

Cover illustration by Malane Newman
Edited by Kathleen Strattan
Cover and text design by John Reinhardt Book Design

Legal Notice

John Reinhardt has made every effort to make sure that the original information provided in this book is accurate as of the date of publication. All information in this book is provided for educational and entertainment purposes only. No warranties of any kind are declared or implied. By reading this book, the reader acknowledges that John Reinhardt is not engaged in rendering legal, financial, or professional advice and that under no circumstances is he responsible for any injuries, damages or losses that are incurred, directly or indirectly, from any suggestions or information in this book. Please refer to your state's or country's rules of the road for specific motor vehicle laws.

John Reinhardt has no responsibility for the persistence or accuracy of URLs for external or third-party Internet websites referred to in this publication and does not guarantee that any content on such websites is, or will remain, accurate or appropriate.

Printed in the United States of America

To my wife, Lynn,
and my daughter, Kim

Acknowledgments

First of all, thank you to all the police officers who risk their lives every day to protect us on the roads and in life.

Thank you to the First Responders who have to deal with the unnecessary results of incompetent driving.

Thank you to my wife, Lynn, for everything. She patiently listens when I point out bad driving behaviors.

Thank you to my daughter, Kim. She was the "driving force" behind fine-tuning my good driving habits over the years, including while I taught her to drive.

Thank you to Kathleen Strattan and Deb Strubel, whose superior editing, enthusiasm, and support for this project have been priceless.

Thank you to Malane Newman. Her incredible illustration is showcased on this book's cover.

Thank you to my big sister, Jeanne Doob, who's always been there for me.

Thank you to Chris Overbeck, Ken Cheline, Jeff Powers, and Harv Treat for their helpful feedback.

Thank you to Stephen D. Stanley (Assistant Chief, Lexington Fayette Urban County Police Department, retired), Jeff Griggs (Captain, Plant

City, Florida, Fire and Rescue), and Michael Esslinger (author of *Alcatraz: The History of the Penitentiary Years*, *Escaping Alcatraz*, *Letters from Alcatraz*, *James Whitey Bulger*, and *I Want It Now! A Memoir of Life on the Set of Willy Wonka and the Chocolate Factory*), for sharing their experiences.

Contents

Introduction

I am not a licensed or professional driving instructor. I simply love to drive. Therefore, the suggestions I present in this book are based on my driving experiences and reading countless books and articles on driving safety.

Let's begin with my driving history. At 16, it took me two attempts to get my driver's license. At the end of my first attempt, the instructor told me to turn right on the next road. There wasn't a stop sign, so naturally, I didn't stop. I was tricked by a stop sign positioned in the median to the left of the road. I passed the test on my second attempt the following week. A year later, a stop sign was placed on the right side of the road!

Over the next two years, I would get a ticket for running a red light (I swear the yellow light lasted less than a second!), speeding (doing 35 in a 30), and not using my turn signal when changing lanes. A speeding ticket on my motorcycle (this was legit!) ended up with me losing my license for six months.

I had a couple of minor traffic accidents (neither of them my fault) that same year. When I was 18, I was nearly killed on my motorcycle when a driver backed out from a blind driveway. I was lucky to have survived that one!

It was a rough beginning to my "driving career," but I learned the importance of driving seriously and defensively through all that. I made it a point to really learn how to drive.

It has been 55 years and an estimated one million miles of driving since my last ticket, accident, or fender-bender. Over the years, I have studied the art of driving and have kept notes about the bad driving habits I have seen.

As a result of all those years and miles, I am sharing with you 101 wrong, inappropriate, dangerous, discourteous, illegal, and just plain stupid things people do when driving a motor vehicle. Unfortunately, we can't stop others from doing these things, but we can certainly be aware of these behaviors and be prepared to avoid the dangerous situations they can create.

We can also take it upon ourselves to be better drivers and do the right thing!

Let's strive to be better drivers and do the right thing!

Develop Good Driving Habits

Before getting into bad driving habits, we need to talk about good ones.

All drivers should know the rules of the road. While we hope others will follow them, and drive safely and carefully, we should always be prepared for the opposite to happen. This is key to developing safe driving habits. We know what we should do, but what do we do when others aren't driving correctly?

This book will help you recognize these dangerous driving behaviors, what to do to avert problems caused by these drivers, and how to avoid doing them yourself. With these tools, you should be able to enjoy many safe years of driving.

Did you know? In 2019, there were 228,679,719 licensed drivers and 299,267,114 registered vehicles in the United States. These drivers drove a total of 3,261,772,000,000 (over three trillion) miles. (NHTSA, 2021) (Source: https://driving-tests.org/driving-statistics/)

Anticipate every scenario and create options. Knowing potential problems and creating a plan will save your life and maybe someone else's. I believe driving a motor vehicle is a dangerous and potentially life-threatening activity that should be performed in such a way as to not force others to compensate for your driving. Take it seriously. It's a privilege, not a right.

Did you know?

- Average number of car accidents in the .U.S. every year is 6 million.
- More than 90 people die in car accidents everyday.
- 3 million people in the U.S. are injured every year in car accidents.
- Around 2 million drivers in car accidents experience permanent injuries every year.

(Source: https://www.driverknowledge.com/car-accident-statistics/)

Everything we can do to make our roads safer and more enjoyable will benefit us all.

Drive Safely, Drive Defensively!

Challenge

As you read through the book, record how many of these topics you see drivers do, including yourself, by marking the checkboxes before each topic on the Contents page.

After you've read the book, and you know what to look for, challenge your friends to see who can spot the most. Feel free to let me know how many you've seen. There are a lot of them, so I doubt you'll see them all anytime soon. But given time, you might!

Also, if you see any bad driving habits or situations not mentioned in this book, let me know by emailing me at john@bookdesign.com. I'll make note of them and possibly include them in the next edition and give you credit.

Be sure to check out the book's website at youredrivingmecrazy.com.

Let's Hit the Road!

Tailgating

Get off my ass! This one *really* drives me crazy! It's my number one dangerous driving habit.

I talk about keeping proper distance from other drivers later in the book, but tailgating is such a serious offense it demands to have its own section, right up front.

Tailgating is driving so close to the car ahead you reduce your ability to stop in time to prevent a collision.

Tailgating forces the driver ahead to pay more attention to what's behind than what's in front, making an accident more likely. Then if you're right up on his bumper, you can't help crashing into him.

A tailgater might just be thoughtless and immature, nervous and excited about where they're going, not meaning any harm. But they sure look like jerks to others. It's a good way to get a reputation as a poor driver.

Even if the tailgater doesn't cause an accident, eventually they'll tailgate the wrong person, a rageaholic spoiling for confrontation. We've all read the stories about what can happen then.

I'm sure you don't tailgate, right? Good, I didn't think so.

Did you know? Tailgating is among the leading causes of motor vehicle accidents in the United States. According to the National Highway Traffic Safety Administration (NHTSA), following a vehicle too closely causes over 30 percent of all rear-end collisions. Every year close to one million injuries and 2,000 deaths are caused by tailgating. The state with the most tailgating violations is Idaho with 76 drivers cited for tailgating per 10,000 motorists, followed by Georgia, Nebraska, Utah, and Virginia. (Source: https://blog.appwinit.com/is-tailgating-illegal/)

What should you do if you're the one being tailgated?

Don't be tempted to react negatively to the other driver—no dirty looks, no flipping the bird. I know this is asking a lot, but if they're willing to put your and their lives at stake, they might be ready to do anything.

If you're driving the speed limit, try to ignore them. If possible, create an opportunity for the tailgater to pass you. If they won't, try to shake them off by turning at the next exit, pulling over to another lane, or when it's safe, to the side of the road.

If they continue to ride your ass, get off at the next exit and pull into a service station, or someplace where there are others to get help. Safety first!

Proper Driving Distance

I need some space here! A typical definition of proper driving distance is:

> "The operator of a motor vehicle shall not follow another vehicle more closely than is reasonable and prudent, having due regard for the speed of such vehicle and the traffic upon and the condition of the highway." (Wisconsin rules of the road, sect: 346.14)

Remember to always give yourself options. Keeping a safe distance behind the car in front of you gives you the option of braking quickly or maneuvering to either side.

The rule of thumb I've used for many years is one car length for every 10 mph. That may seem excessive at times. And you can certainly modify it according to the road and weather conditions.

Another guideline for safe distance is the "three-second rule," which is driving three seconds behind the car ahead.

There's no reason to drive too close to the car in front of you. Proper distance gives you time to react to a sudden need to brake. It will also provide room for others who need to slip into that space to avoid a different situation.

Left Laners

Hey, this isn't Scotland! It's very simple here in the U.S.—the right lane is for driving, the left lane is for passing. If you aren't passing, get in the right lane! Come on!

Did you know? While most states do have laws about which lane you drive in, there are eight states where it's illegal to drive in the left lane except for turning left or passing. They are: Illinois, Kansas, Kentucky, Louisiana, Maine, Massachusetts, New Jersey, and West Virginia. (AutoInsurance.org, https://www.autoinsurance.org/keep-right-which-states-enforce-left-lane-passing-only/#:~:text=As%20you%20can%20see%2C%20most,New%20Jersey%2C%20and%20West%20Virginia)

When someone is driving in the left lane and should be in the right lane, it's obvious they're not aware of anyone around them. So be careful, because they probably don't even know you're behind them.

A driver coming up at a higher rate of speed behind a slow driver in the left lane must often make a dangerous move to get around the vehicle in the left lane.

I can justify driving in the left lane (*as long as you're not impeding traffic from behind*) for the following reasons:

- The right lane is under construction.
- The right lane pavement is really bad.
- There's bumper-to-bumper traffic and you have no choice.
- The weather has created a safer surface in the left lane.
- There's an accident or emergency vehicle on the right side of the road.
- You're preparing to turn left ahead.
- You're passing.

Otherwise, stay out of the left lane. It's the "right" thing to do.

Variable Driving Speeds

Do you have commitment issues? Do you walk at various speeds? I doubt it. There are enough things to concentrate on while driving without dealing with someone in front of you speeding up and slowing down.

I'm amused (frustrated is more like it) by people who pass me, and then slow down, so I pass them, and then they speed up and pass me again, all while I'm driving the same speed.

And how about drivers who speed up when you try to pass them? Or slow down after they pass and get in front of you?

Sometimes uneven driving indicates distraction, such as being impaired, on the phone, wearing earbuds, or anything else that will cause the driver to unknowingly alter their speed. At best, it's just a bad habit that needs to be consciously broken.

Our cars are equipped with a cool feature—cruise control—which may give you better gas mileage. When on the highway, use your cruise control when possible. Fluctuating speeds cause problems for other drivers and can provoke road rage in those behind you.

Be patient with people slowing down on uphills and curves. It's frustrating, but maybe their car isn't up to par, or they aren't as familiar with the local roads as you are. And be mindful of maintaining your own (appropriate, safe) speed when going uphill and around curves.

Driving at a consistent speed allows others to focus on other things around them, creating a safer environment for all of us.

So pick a speed and stick to it.

Merging

May I cut in? My two issues here are how some people merge onto the main road from a ramp and when they merge into the passing lane.

The Cambridge Dictionary defines merge as:

> "To join a line of moving traffic without causing other vehicles to slow down."

My first beef: when people merge into interstate traffic at a slow speed. Interstate traffic, in most cases, is 55 to 75 mph. Slow entry causes everyone to adjust, change lanes, and/or slow down. (For a more substantial rant on this, see "Entering an Interstate Too Slowly.")

> **Did you know?** Over 500,000 accidents occur each year as a result of improper lane changes and merges. (U.S. Department of Transportation)

My second beef: when drivers abruptly veer into the passing lane. They don't use turn signals; they don't assume the speed of the traffic in the passing lane (notice how I refer to the left lane as the passing lane—because that's what it's for!); and they don't accurately gauge the distance of the cars with which they're merging.

Okay, folks, here is my lesson for safe and proper merging into the passing lane:

- **Anticipate** the time you'll need to pull into the passing lane due to the speed you're approaching the vehicle in front of you.
- **Start looking in your mirrors** to see what traffic is already in the passing lane and how fast they're approaching you.
- **Wait until there's plenty of room** in the left lane and you still have distance between yourself and the vehicle in front of you.
- **Turn on your turn signal** in advance of actual merging, giving others plenty of notice as to your intentions.
- At the right time, **begin your merge** by reaching the speed of the traffic already in the passing lane.
- After you can clearly see the vehicle you've just passed in your inside rearview mirror, take a **look back to your right and left** to make sure you're clear.
- Make a **safe return to the driving lane**.

Remember, you should drive so as not to force others to compensate for your poor driving.

Trapping on Merge

Nope, they just can't let you in! You don't exist! There are too many clowns on the road who feel like they own the space in front of their car, leaving you stuck in the merge line. Why is it so important to prevent someone from merging into the lane in front of you?

From the perspective of the driver merging onto the interstate, it's frustrating when a car or truck insists on staying in the right lane, even when the left lane is clear. You generally have to slow way down to get on, leaving you entering the interstate at a less-than-desirable speed.

When you're the one on the interstate approaching an entrance ramp, either get over to the left lane or position yourself (speed up or slow down) to create a space for the incoming cars. This takes some anticipation on your part by looking to see what traffic is in the lane next to you.

There's also the situation where people need to merge into your lane (closed lane, exit ramp, emergency vehicle, etc.). Instead of merging in advance, making a smooth merge for everyone, they rush to the front and merge at the last possible moment, forcing you to slow down to let them in.

Merge signs are generally provided with advance notice to give us all time to make speed adjustments.

Let's work together and get to our destinations safely.

Merging at the Last Minute

Threading a needle? You see a merge sign ahead. Scan all your mirrors to see what opportunity you have to merge. Then turn on your signal and try to merge as soon as you know it's safe.

Don't wait till the last minute. This comes across to other drivers as rude and inconsiderate. As described in the topic above, too many people rush to the front of the line, creating a jam and forcing those behind to fall farther back in order.

As much as you might be frustrated by the wait time, be patient. Your chance will soon come.

Driving Over the Center Line

Pick a lane, please! Unless you're passing someone, there's an obstacle in the road, you're stupid drunk, or you're a terrible driver, there's no reason to drive over the center line while going straight. Regardless, I see this all the time.

I know, I know, you have other things to do and think about besides driving and keeping the car within your lane. It's just too much work to actually "drive" the car. Yeah, the vehicle just drifts, and you have to pull it back now and then to keep it going straight.

If you can't keep your car within the generous driving space provided, you shouldn't be driving.

Keep the car between the lines or you're going to kill someone.

Lane Weaving

To and fro, which way doth thee wend? There's a lot of weaving going on these days with the use of cell phones, lazy driving, and paying attention to everything but driving.

Weaving used to be the sign of an impaired driver. Today, it can indicate anything, including simply being a sloppy or immature driver.

Weaving back and forth across lanes requires the other drivers to compensate, and it can cause accidents.

The best thing to do is get past weaving drivers as quickly and safely as possible. Better to have this driver behind you than in front of you.

The lines are there for a reason. So, stay focused and stay between them.

Turn Signals

Is it a secret? Could you at least give us a clue?

These are the seven reasons why I think people don't use turn signals:

- It doesn't affect them (so they think).
- They know where they're going.
- They don't want you to know.
- They don't know where they're going.
- Laziness.
- Their turn signals or lights aren't working.
- Lack of consideration for others.

The use of turn signals is undoubtedly a safety factor, but also a simple courtesy. Letting people know what you're doing allows others to make adjustments and prepare for what they're going to do.

Use turn signals EVERY TIME you're going to turn the car: parking lots, changing lanes, pulling over, etc. Let others know what you're going to do. It is commonly recommended to turn on your signal 100 feet in advance of the turn when driving in town.

Often, drivers turn their signal on, but don't turn it off (see "Turn Signals on for Several Turns"). I've also seen many times when someone turns in the opposite direction of their turn signal! So always take other drivers' turn signals with a grain of salt. Pay attention to them, but don't trust them completely.

Make using turn signals a habit—but turn them off after you've turned.

Lack of Maintenance

You really don't care, do you? This is a real problem. Automobiles that aren't mechanically safe are a danger to the driver and passengers, and everyone around them. Unsafe vehicles can't operate properly or react to emergencies. We don't need to be dodging the parts falling off your car or truck! And mechanical issues are often the cause of car fires.

> **Did you know?** According to federal government statistics, about 2% of car accidents are caused by mechanical failure. Typically, the failure stems from inadequate maintenance or faulty parts. (Source: https://crashstats.nhtsa.dot.gov/Api/Public/ViewPublication/812115)

If the car isn't maintained, it's likely the driver isn't up to par, either, and doesn't care. As I keep saying throughout this book, steer clear of these cars and drivers.

Items on Dashboard or Back Panel

Imagine what their house looks like! You'll see many people put stuffed animals and other items on the back shelf of their cars. You'll also notice many work truck vehicles with papers, lunch, hats, and other items on the dashboard. This is dangerous. If the car has to stop suddenly, those items become projectiles and may injure passengers or cause the driver to lose control.

Having things on the floorboard may also create a situation where something would roll underneath your brake pedal and not allow you to stop.

There are plenty of spaces in the car to keep things secure.

Turn Right on Red Without Stopping

So, you saved three seconds? You'll notice many people who choose to slow down at a red light or stop sign only to see if they have to stop. Rather than stopping to see if they can go.

When going through an intersection, keep your eyes on pedestrians and oncoming traffic from the right. Watch for anyone who looks like they're not going to stop at the light.

A few related notes:

Not all intersections allow turning on red.

Left turns on red into a one-way street, even from a two-way street, are allowed in most states unless signs prohibit such a turn. Know the laws where you're driving, and obey them.

And finally, as I learned the hard way when I failed my first driving test, look for the signs posted. They're not always in the place you expect.

Headlights

It's good to be seen! Unfortunately, most people believe headlights should only be used at night. This is wrong. Always use your headlights. It's much easier to see an oncoming car when its lights are on.

Like turn signals, headlights are for the benefit of others as well as yourself. Headlights allow others to see you at night, in fog, in the rain, and at a distance. And your headlights always help other drivers see you sooner, giving them more time to adjust accordingly.

Most new cars have an auto setting for the headlights to be on at all times, so you don't have to think about it.

Not only are headlights important, but the taillights are as well. Driving behind a car without lighted taillights in the fog, for instance, creates a dangerous situation.

Please make sure your headlights are on at all times—and make sure they're not on bright (except for rural driving when there aren't other cars coming toward you).

One more thing. Some cars have plastic headlight covers (lenses) that will develop a cloudy film on them over time. This will prevent the headlights from effectively and safely lighting the road. Check yours and either clean or replace them. It's worth it.

Indicator Lamps

But I had the turn signal on, officer! Unless there's an indicator on the dashboard alerting to a failed bulb, most people don't pay attention to the status of their headlights and taillights. This can cause a situation where you turn on your turn signal, but since the light isn't working, the other driver assumes you're going straight. An avoidable accident occurs.

This goes back to keeping your car mechanically safe. While you can't see your brake lights and turn signals from inside the car, it's important that other drivers do. Make sure your lights are always working properly.

And never count too much on another driver's brake lights or turn signals to tell you when and whether they're going to stop or turn.

Sudden Stops

Whoa, Nelly! Anticipate stopping at ALL times. Drivers with their heads in the clouds won't be ready for unexpected stops. The possibility of sudden braking by the car in front of you is another reason to keep proper distance. This is where tailgaters will find themselves in a rear-end accident.

And as you'll keep hearing me say, brakes are the most important feature of your car. You want them to work when you need them.

Speeding

Speed kills! Here we go! Speeding ranks right up there with tailgating as one of the most dangerous driving habits. Most people don't have the driving skills to operate their vehicles at the speed limit, let alone when they're going too fast.

Speeding increases the risk of an accident, reducing the response time for the speeder and those around them.

A speed limit is imposed for good reason, to ensure safe driving conditions on that particular section of road.

Did you know? In 2018, speeding was the cause of 31% of motorcyclist fatalities, 18% of car driver fatalities, 14% of light-truck driver fatalities, and 7% of large-truck driver fatalities. (US Department of Transportation, 2020) (Source: https://driving-tests.org/driving-statistics/)

Don't be in a hurry for a ticket or an accident. And watch for others who are speeding, driving too fast for weather/road conditions, or driving too fast for the kind of vehicle they have, and the shape it's in. Stay away from those drivers.

Driving Too Slow

It's slow motion! The flip side of driving too fast is driving too slowly.

Driving too slowly can be nearly as dangerous as speeding. Driving too slowly will force cars to brake unexpectedly and possibly force them to change lanes quickly to avoid the slow driver.

This can create a chain reaction of accidents.

Watch ahead for slow drivers, plan your moves accordingly, and drive with the speed of traffic.

Going Too Fast for Conditions

Hey, watch this! Too many people like to drive fast. I get it. But do that on a racetrack, not on the road. Driving too fast is risky for you and others, even more so in bad weather conditions. We've all read about fatal accidents that happened like this, even if we're fortunate enough not to personally know anyone who was killed that way.

When it's foggy, raining, snowy, at night, and on roads in need of repair, drive at a responsible speed to minimize the risk of an accident.

And this bears repeating—stay away from those who are driving faster than everyone else. Give them a wide berth.

Side Roads

Ready or not, here I come! Not only do you need to keep your eyes on the road in front of you and the cars around you, but you also need to watch side roads. And not just side roads you can see, but roads around curves, driveways, and roads and driveways hidden by cars (see my motorcycle accident described in the Introduction), trees, bushes, signs, and buildings.

Many times, drivers will misjudge the time it takes to pull out into the road safely and will pull out right in front of you.

Conversely, sometimes other drivers will wait longer than needed when they easily could have pulled out sooner. If you ever find yourself behind a more hesitant driver like this (and you will) and need to wait an extra minute, be kind, be patient. Don't blow the horn. You'll be on your way soon.

Multitasking

Why not just catch up on your sleep while you're driving? When you're behind the wheel of an automobile, you have one job—get you, your passengers, the automobile, and other drivers to the destinations safely. Focus only on driving.

Don't try to do other things while you're driving. Wait till you get where you're going. Or pull over. Or ask a passenger to do the task for you.

Did you know? Over 80% of drivers admit to dangerous behavior while driving, such as changing clothes, steering with a foot, painting nails, or even shaving. (TeenSafe, 2018) (Source: https://driving-tests.org/driving-statistics/)

Those who are doing more things than simply driving aren't going to be able to react properly to a situation that comes up suddenly. And they're likely to cause an accident.

So please wait until you can stop the car to shave, read, text, talk on the phone, apply makeup, and do everything else people seem to think they can do while driving.

Parking

Split the difference! This is another one of my many pet peeves. There are lines in a parking lot for a reason, to indicate where to park. Too many people park too close to the lines, park over the lines, don't pull in far enough, or pull in too far.

If you get out of your car and notice you've overshot the lines, it's okay to get back in your car and make adjustments to get in the right spot. In fact, please do so!

If you can't park your car between two lines, you probably shouldn't be driving between the two on the road.

Tires

Where the rubber meets the road! Do you wear sandals when walking on snow or ice? There are many cars on the road with worn tires in need of replacement. Tires are the direct contact with the road. Making sure the tires are appropriate for the road conditions, adequately inflated, and have good tread will help them perform as expected in emergencies.

Did you know? Some 11,000 accidents occur every year due to bad tires, according to the National Highway Traffic Safety Administration (NHTSA). Moreover, dangerous driving conditions from winter weather and driving on worn tires are two of the most common causes for vehicle collisions. (Source: https://www.automotive-fleet.com/10161436/safety-tips-bad-tires-cause-11-000-accidents-annually#:~:text=Some%2011%2C000%20accidents%20occur%20every,common%20causes%20for%20vehicle%20collisions./)

And be on the lookout for other cars with worn tires. They won't be able to brake quickly and might cause a slide.

Also, summer tires don't work well on snow. The extra cost of winter tires will be well worth it when they help you maneuver on wintry roads, and save you the higher cost of an accident.

Spinning Tires, Throwing Rocks

What, are you ten years old? When driving on gravel roads, make sure you keep a good distance behind the car in front of you. Rocks are flying at all times, whether you know it or not. They can crack your windshield, chip the paint, and distract you.

This is especially important at a stop sign. The car in front of you may suddenly lurch forward, throwing rocks up onto your vehicle.

So watch the drivers in front of you to see what kind of driving habits they have. Adjust your distance accordingly.

Also, braking and maneuvering on gravel roads are tricky as your car won't perform the same as it does on paved roads.

And some dangerous skids can happen on paved roads when there's gravel sprinkled on top of the pavement. Avoid speeding and sudden braking that might throw you into a spin.

Bad Weather Driving

What's the difference? Too many people don't adjust their driving in bad weather. Weather conditions affect your ability to stop and maneuver the car. You'll need more braking distance.

In bad weather, everyone should slow down. (See also "Going Too Fast for Conditions.") Be extra vigilant. Create more space around you.

Everything changes while driving in snow, rain, ice, fog, hail, strong wind, etc. This is where good habits will go a long way toward keeping you and others safe.

Squeezing Into Your Safe Space

Hey, did you forget I'm here? Sometimes that safe space you've created in front of you is an opportunity for someone else to pull in. This frequently occurs in traffic and can happen quickly and unexpectedly. (See also "Cutting Off.")

When some idiot squeezes in, back off as quickly as you can and create the needed space. This is one of the many reasons why it's important to keep a safe driving distance from the car in front of you in case you need to brake suddenly.

Turn Signals on for Several Turns

At least they're using the turn signal! Just because the car in front of you has its turn signal on, doesn't mean it's turning at the next available turning point.

First, the driver may not even know the signal is on.

Second, they may pass one or more turns before finally making the intended turn.

It's frustrating for sure. But the driver might be lost, or unfamiliar with the local roads. Just be patient and don't be too sure ahead of time which turn they will make. This rule applies both to a car in front of you and a car coming toward you.

Bright Lights

Am I on television? Most cars today have an auto-dimming feature that will automatically dim your lights for oncoming vehicles.

Many people have no idea their lights are on bright, even though there's a bright light indicator on the dash—another reason to continually monitor the instrument panel.

If someone has their brights on behind you, the best thing you can do is adjust your mirrors.

If the car is coming at you, don't look directly at the lights. Some people will flash their lights at someone with brights on. This isn't a good idea, as doing so can aggravate someone who might take it the wrong way and turn around and become aggressive.

Slowing Down Long Before the Light

You can't wait to catch up on my texts? Upon approaching a red light, some drivers slow down or simply stop early. Then, when they have finished their text (or whatever they're in a hurry to do), they gradually make their way to the intersection. This is happening more these days because of cell phones. A car stops a couple of car lengths behind the vehicle in front, waits a minute, and then gradually pulls up to the proper spot. So many drivers are in a hurry to stop to read their texts.

This is annoying because instead of coming to a stop at normal speed and having time to rest from driving, you have to creep along behind this person. There isn't much you can do but follow them to the final stopping point.

When stopping at a light or stop sign, pull up behind the car in front of you to where you can still see their rear tires.

Crossing the Lane to Avoid Something

What the heck was that?! If you're faced with a situation where you have to cross over the center line because of a parked vehicle, something in the road, or issues with the road itself, you should slow down, turn on your signal, prepare to stop if necessary, and cross into the other lane ONLY when it's safe.

Too many times, I have to come to a stop because an oncoming car just swerves out into my lane to avoid slowing or stopping in their lane.

The issue is in their lane, not mine! They should be the ones making the adjustments, not me!

Parking on the Road

The road is not for parking! Parking in a traffic lane isn't appropriate unless there's an emergency. And if it's an emergency, flashing warning lights should be used. Otherwise, drive to the nearest parking space.

I have seen many times in Boston where people simply stop on the road. That's right, stop and get out, leaving their car right there on the road. Maybe these people don't want to be inconvenienced by having to park somewhere down the road, though they're fine with you being inconvenienced.

There are two things you can do. Turn on your flashers and wait for the driver of the car to come back out and move the car. Or use your turn signal and wait for a safe time to pass. The drivers behind you can't see why you're stopped, so immediately applying your flashers or turn signal will indicate you're not the problem.

Items Hanging From the Mirror

It's not a Christmas tree! Keep your eye out for drivers who have things hanging from their rear-view mirror. The windshield was designed to give you a clear view of everything in front of you. Those fuzzy dice hanging from your mirror will only impede your vision.

In time, you'll get used to the motion of those items, preventing you from recognizing a moving vehicle or pedestrian.

If you have a handicap tag, please hang it only when parked. It has no purpose while you're driving and will obstruct your view.

Mirrors

To see or not to see? That is the question. We have mirrors for a purpose. I know, to apply lipstick, comb hair, and check to see if your teeth are clean of food.

Seriously, if you constantly check the three mirrors, you will significantly increase your chances of a safe outing.

When stopped behind a car in traffic, you should be able to see their face in both their driver's side mirror and center mirror. If not, and this is important, they can't see you!

You need to be aware of everything going on in front of you, around you, and behind you.

Make sure you check and adjust all three mirrors every time you get into the car. And, as I've mentioned before (see "Multitasking"), you shouldn't use the mirrors for grooming tasks like shaving, hair-combing, and applying makeup while driving.

Using Your Phone

Hang up, people! This has become a real problem. When you're talking or texting with someone on the phone, your mind is focused on what you're saying or writing. You're not paying attention to your driving and what's around you.

As of this writing, 48 states have bans on texting while driving. The law varies from state to state, so please check your state's rules for details.

And please, refrain from using your phone while driving. If you must, pull over! It's not only the safe thing for you, but everyone else on the road!

Many new cars allow use of your phone through a wireless connection, enabling you to talk without holding or focusing on the phone. While this is acceptable in cases of emergency, it's best to get in the habit of waiting until you're safely stopped to make calls and texts.

The phone is now the number one cause of vehicle accidents. Life is too precious!

Impaired Driving

I only had one drink, officer! There isn't much I can say here that hasn't already been said, and continues to be said through ads, billboards, public service announcements, and even by the manufacturers of alcohol themselves. There's no upside to this. The more you drink or ingest, the more your reaction time, senses, and judgment are altered, resulting in an increased likelihood of an accident.

Impaired driving is not limited to alcohol. Drugs, marijuana, and even prescription drugs can put you in a state not suitable for driving a car.

The biggest challenge is when you're drunk, or high, you're likely to believe you're okay to drive. Well, you're not. If you don't have a sober designated driver, call a friend, a family member, or a commercial service to drive you home.

Courtesy

Be kind, be happy! Be courteous when you drive. Isn't it exhilarating to be part of the traffic on those days when cooperation and coordination among all the drivers feel like a symphony, and it seems like everyone's in a friendly mood?

Do things for other drivers you'd like done for you. (Hmmm... that sounds familiar, doesn't it?) If you see someone trying to enter traffic, and you can let them in without impeding those behind you, do so. This sounds simple but is huge in its impact. Give more than you take. Allow people to merge, enter from side roads, turn ahead of you, etc. We're all in this together!

When someone gestures for you to go ahead of them, wave and thank them. And when someone doesn't acknowledge your kind action, no worries, plenty of other people will. You've done the right thing.

Reading and Driving

Are you that bored? Speaking of multitasking, people do actually read and drive. Even before cell phones, many people would read the newspaper on their way to work!

Yep, apparently reading the news, which can wait, is more important than avoiding the accident they're going to cause.

Now people are reading their phones. Watch people as you approach and pass to see if they're watching the road or reading. You'll be surprised!

Throwing Trash

Keep it in the car! Yes, after all these years, the money spent on advertising, the signs threatening fines, and the general concern for our environment, some still throw garbage from their cars. It's hard to believe, right? I feel sorry for those who have to work or live with these people. Just imagine the other boorish things they do every day.

It is illegal in most states to throw trash from your car. The driver is responsible for this action.

Did you know? In Florida, littering is a crime. People who throw trash on public streets and highways can be fined up to $500 or jailed up to 60 days. You can be charged with a first-degree misdemeanor and fined up to $1,000 if dumping more than 15 pounds of trash. The court may also require you to pick up litter along roadways. (Source: https://www.stateofflorida.com/driving-privilege/)

Please, if you have garbage in your car, wait until you arrive at your destination to dispose of it properly.

Throwing Cigarettes Out of the Window

The world is not an ashtray! Some people evidently think of the outdoors as one giant ashtray, but they likely don't realize filters on cigarettes are made of a form of plastic and can take as long as 10 years to decompose. If you've done this, not realizing it was littering, I won't tell anyone—since now that you know, you won't do it again, right? That goes for discarding cigarette butts on the sidewalk while walking, too.

Another serious problem here is when you're driving with your windows down, a thrown cigarette from a car ahead of you can easily find its way into your vehicle, or onto the bed of your pickup truck, starting a fire there (an anecdote from real life). Watch for smoke coming out of the windows of the cars ahead.

Did you know? According to the North Carolina Department of Public Safety:

- Tobacco products make up more than one third of existing litter.
- A discarded cigarette butt takes 12 years to break down and leaks cadmium, lead and arsenic into soil and waterways.
- Cigarette butts can poison children or animals who may find and eat them.
- Cigarette butts that accumulate outside of buildings, on parking lots or streets can be washed through storm drains to streams, rivers, and beaches.
- Lit cigarettes thrown from car windows can cause forest fires.

(Source: https://www.ncdps.gov/dps-services/crime-prevention/litter-free-nc/litter-facts)

And finally, cigarettes tossed out onto dry grass have the potential to start a fire that can spread quickly and result in catastrophic loss.

If you're going to smoke in your car, put the cigarette out in your car's ashtray.

Cutting Off

Get out of my way, I'm coming through! Cutting off, along with tailgating and speeding, is one of the most dangerous moves in driving. The ripple effect of such a move can cause a series of accidents.

If you're not aware of the cars around you and don't anticipate being cut off, you may suddenly have to brake or swerve when someone cuts in front of you, causing those behind you to suddenly react.

While the person cutting you off is certainly at fault, your preparation can prevent something serious from happening.

Like so many of these situations, watching the cars around you and their behavior may give you clues as to what these drivers will do when they get near you.

Attachments to the Vehicle

Catch it and you keep it! I'm talking about pickup trucks with items in the back, cars with ski racks, luggage racks, bicycles tied on the back of the vehicle, trailers carrying objects, etc.

These items are potential projectiles. It's not uncommon for them to detach, causing a potentially tragic chain of events.

If possible, try to ride to the side of these vehicles and not directly behind.

If objects are in an open truck bed, and you can't pass, keep extra distance to give you time to react if an item were to fly out.

Like many situations mentioned in this book, being aware of what's around you and your options can save a life, or at least prevent some serious damage.

One more thing: make sure your own attached items are secure before hitting the road.

Blocking View at an Intersection

I'd like to see clearly now! This is an inconsiderate move people may be making without being aware of it: while waiting to turn left at an intersection, many people will come up to the right of you to turn right. They pull out so far that they block your view of oncoming traffic from your right. This forces you to wait until they turn so you can see clearly.

If you're going to turn right and there's a car waiting next to you to turn left, either stay behind them (taking your turn as if they were there first), or pull out far enough so they can see behind your car.

Too Old to Drive

Time to retire the keys. For many people, giving up the ability to drive is one of life's most difficult decisions. Many feel a loss of independence. But what's more important—the loss of independence or the loss of life?

If you are close to someone who has shown continual examples of why they shouldn't be driving, don't hesitate to pursue this subject. I sympathize that it's easier said than done. Below are some suggestions, to be served with all the tact and kindness you can muster:

- Have conversations with them and ask them to stop driving.
- Provide proof they're not a safe and competent driver.

- Have a family meeting.
- Consult their doctor.
- Suggest alternate means of transportation (which you have researched for them—and all the better if you have the time and inclination to drive them where they need to go).

And if people have expressed concern about *your* driving, or you're regularly involved in accidents—major or minor—please be open to accepting that it's time for you to stop driving.

Did you know? 6,549 people 65 and older killed in traffic crashes in 2020—17% of all traffic fatalities. (Source: US Department of Transportation, https://www.nhtsa.gov/road-safety/older-drivers)

Talk with your family doctor to get advice for yourself (if you're wondering if you should hang up the car keys), and/or to have the doctor talk with the person with whom you have this concern. It might be easier for your family member to accept if he hears it from the doctor, rather than from you.

Giving up the car keys may be hard and inconvenient, but it's sometimes the right thing to do.

Over-55 Drivers

In some states, mature drivers can get insurance discounts for taking driver improvement courses every few years. Save a buck and save a life. American Automobile Association (AAA) and American Association of Retired Persons (AARP) both offer them, and there are some others. Check out the ones recommended by your state's Department of Transportation. You can take them online or in person, depending on the course. They're inexpensive, take about a day to complete, and are well worth your time. Even though I'm sure you're already an excellent driver, you're bound to come away with a few new good habits.

Stopped at a Green Light

Go! Are you sleeping? While this isn't a serious infraction, it does create frustration for others. More and more these days, drivers are quick to look at their phones at the earliest opportunity. Stop lights are common for this. And so, you'll probably see someone sitting at a green light or stop sign longer than expected.

Likewise, as you approach an intersection you may encounter those who hesitate or simply wait through their turn.

When approaching an intersection, refrain from looking at your phone. Begin to look at the intersecting corners. Determine when it's your turn. The first to arrive is the first to go. If two vehicles arrive at the same time, the vehicle to the right has the right-of-way. Be ready when it's your turn to proceed. Be patient, be cautious, but be decisive.

Young Drivers

It's cool to be a good driver! Young drivers can be a serious problem on the road, having yet to develop experience, maturity, and the ability to reason quickly and soundly. There are many things to know about driving and it's important that the young driver be ready for this adult responsibility.

Did you know? Globally, car accidents are the leading cause of death among young adults ages 15–29—and the ninth leading cause of death for all people. (SaferAmerica, 2019) (Source: https://driving-tests.org/driving-statistics/)

Driving can be fun in a safe and controlled environment. But when you have cars whizzing at you, by you, and around you, bad things can happen very quickly.

Did you know? Drivers aged 25 to 34 are the deadliest age group in 32 states. (Source: https://www.autoinsurance.org/age-groups-fatal-crashes/)

As we said in Boy Scouts, Be Prepared. I am hopeful this book will help young drivers learn to watch for situations they wouldn't otherwise.

Did you know? Teens are more likely than older drivers to underestimate or not be able to recognize dangerous situations. Teens are also more likely than adults to make critical errors that can lead to serious crashes. (Source: https://www.cdc.gov/transportationsafety/teen_drivers/teendrivers_factsheet.html)

Party when you get there! In some cases, when there is a car full of young people, the activities within in the car create a distraction for the driver, causing the driver to pay more attention to the fun than what's going on outside the vehicle.

Keep an eye out for cars filled with young people and pay attention to their actions.

Going Straight in Turn-Only Lane

Sorry, changed my mind! There are times when suddenly you find yourself in a turn-only lane. Some roads are marked clearly, but if the traffic is heavy, and you're in an unfamiliar place, you may not realize the lane is turn-only until you near the intersection.

Don't veer suddenly into an adjacent, non-turning lane, cutting off another driver. They expect you to turn and are basing their actions on that assumption. Take the hit and turn. It's not a big deal. Turn back to the intersection at your earliest convenience and be on your way—safely.

It's similar if you miss your exit lane in heavy traffic because you can't get over soon enough. Don't just close your eyes and force your way into the exit lane at the last minute, hoping for the best. You don't want to frighten your passengers into fortifying themselves with Jack Daniels and crash helmets whenever they white-knuckle it through a ride with you. Just get off at the next exit, get back on the highway, and give it another try. Eventually, you'll be able to exit safely. Proof: if that weren't true, you'd still be out there, stuck in traffic somewhere, instead of reading this book.

Backing Up Without Looking

Look out! At any given moment, for whatever reason, the car ahead of you may decide to back up. Yes, this happens. Yes, right in the middle of the road. I'm shaking my head, too. Another reason you should be prepared by keeping the proper distance behind. This distance will allow you enough time to react and alert the other driver that you are behind them. Now, this is one occasion where the use of your horn is proper. (For more on backing up without looking, see "Parked Cars" and "Backing Up on the Exit.")

Cutting Across Lanes When Turning

I don't need no stinking lines to tell me where to drive! I'm talking here in particular when there are multiple turn lanes with dotted lines around the turn on the road to direct travel. I'm amazed how many people don't keep their cars within those lines.

It's lazy driving and results in fender-benders. Lazy driving is poor driving.

Entering an Interstate Too Slowly

Excuse me, please! Here you are traveling 70 mph on the interstate. A car at the entrance ramp ahead of you is driving at 55 mph. You can't get over into the left lane, so you must brake. And everyone else behind you has to brake simply because someone doesn't enter the interstate at proper speed.

A friendly reminder here that a Merge sign isn't the same as a Yield sign. It doesn't mean "Stop," or "Slow to a crawl."

As you're traveling along the entrance to the interstate, look at the cars coming up and anticipate your entry point to traffic. Reach that speed before your merge. Turn signal is on, proper speed, and a seamless entry onto the interstate. Well done!

Bicycles

Spinning on the road. Always be on the lookout for bicycles. Cyclists can't see cars behind them very well. And many cyclists don't stay tight to the side of the road and often weave.

If you are driving on a multi-lane road, and there is a car beside you to your right that will soon be coming up on a cyclist, slow down or move over, if you can safely do so, to give the car room to get around the bike.

More roads offer bike lanes and paths these days. Occasionally, bike lanes actually reside in between two car lanes. Please watch for these situations.

Now and then, you will see an idiot riding their bike toward you in your lane. I know, this is crazy, but they're out there! Be prepared to move or stop as the bike approaches. If they're stupid enough to ride against traffic, they might swerve out in front of you.

Pulling Into the Breakdown Lane

Safety first, please! If you can't wait for the next exit and must pull over, get as far off the side of the road as possible.

When we're driving and look at something away from the road, we unknowingly tend to steer in that direction. Parking too close to the road increases the chances of a passing car side-swiping or hitting you directly.

If you must leave the car, do it quickly and carefully. Put on your emergency flashers and move to the safe side of the vehicle. Watch oncoming traffic at all times.

This is important: if you're outside of the car, stand away from the car, never in front of it. If someone swerves and hits your vehicle, you'll be clear of it.

Please do try to wait until there's an exit if you need to stop, though, if possible. This is the safest choice for you and others.

Misaligned Headlights

My lights are on, but I can't see the road! Misaligned headlights fall in the mechanical category, but this is different from a non-working lamp.

Misaligned headlights affect both the driver and oncoming cars. Such misalignment will diminish the lighted view ahead of the vehicle, and it can also create a high beam effect for oncoming traffic.

It's noble to be a do-it-yourselfer, but if you want it done right, fixing your misaligned headlights might be best left to your mechanic.

Following a Car Through a Red Light

Excuse me, I'm with them! Some just can't wait their turn. Their time is more important than yours. Just ask them. No, just watch their actions. Some believe if they follow a car closely enough through a red light, the two cars are as one, somehow making running the red light okay.

Don't do this. Red light means STOP, nothing else. We're even given a yellow warning light that the red light is about to come. There's no excuse for running a red light. Even if you're riding the bumper of the car in front of you, which you shouldn't be.

Rolling Through Stop Signs

Stop, please! Even if you're the only one at an intersection in the middle of nowhere, bad habits can come back to haunt you.

This is a great opportunity for you to develop good driving practices. Make it a habit to come to a complete stop at all stop situations, even if nobody else is around. What does it take, two, three seconds?

Roundabouts

Round and round, where we go, nobody knows! Roundabouts require a lot of concentration. From simple, single-lane roundabouts with two exits to ones with multiple lanes and exits and speeds of 50 mph, it's like jumping onto a merry-go-round. You have to watch traffic entering and exiting from multiple directions, as well as those changing lanes midway through the circle.

Did you know? Nationwide, there are 35% fewer car accidents in roundabouts than in traditional intersections. The Federal Highway Administration says roundabouts can offer up to a 90% reduction in intersection-related fatalities and a 75% reduction in intersection-related injuries. (US Department of Transportation, Federal Highway Administration)

Anticipate in advance where you want your car to be in the circle to make the desired exit. Enter at the speed at which the cars inside the circle are going. Position yourself for the right exit, use turn signals, and exit.

I rarely see turn signals used in roundabouts, though they should be—so anticipate any action by any car.

There are always those who pull into a roundabout going much slower than the traffic. This can cause some serious problems.

It's one thing when everyone is going in a straight line with no exits and entrances, but a roundabout has multiple activities (because everyone in the roundabout is trying to exit) going on at the same time. And the people on the opposite side can't see what your side is doing. So when someone enters slowly, causing others to slow down, look out!

If you're trapped, and can't make your exit, don't panic. Continue to drive through the roundabout, positioning yourself for another try at your exit. You'll get there.

Snow on Car

Snow what? If your windshield is covered with snow, don't just clear enough to see straight ahead. Clear the entire windows, front, sides, and back.

Also, clear any snow on the hood of the car, as this snow will find its way to the windshield when driving. And the snow on the top of the car, so it doesn't slide down to the rear window and fly into the windshield of the car behind you.

Drivers need to have complete visibility, especially in hazardous conditions.

Pay close attention to cars ahead of you as the snow on them is likely to land on your windshield.

This is also true with semis, since the tops of the trailers carry a lot of snow and at any moment that snow can let loose, causing a real problem for drivers behind.

Stopping Short of Stop Light

Do you see an invisible car in front of you? This is more of an inconsideration issue than a dangerous one. If you stop one or two car lengths from the intersection, you're preventing one or two (or more) cars behind you from getting through the intersection in that light sequence. This might cause someone behind you to run a red light.

It may also cause others to think something may be wrong, that you're having car problems or a medical emergency.

Also, there are sensors at many intersections that trigger when a car is present. This affects how the lights change. If you're too far back, the sensor may not trigger, causing a delay in the light change.

Headlights in Rain

Let's play hide and seek! As I keep saying like a broken record, always use your headlights. It's harder to see a vehicle without their headlights on. And you should especially use headlights when visibility is low and in the rain and snow. All three of these situations reduce the distance we can see and be seen, thus cutting reaction time.

Did you know? Headlights must be turned on when it's raining, foggy, snowing, or even cloudy. If you must use your windshield wipers, you are required to have your headlights on. Headlights must be turned on if you cannot see at least 1000 feet in front of you. (Source: https://www.yourmechanic.com/article/headlight-use-laws-for-all-50-states#:~:text=Headlights%20must%20be%20turned%20on,feet%20in%20front%20of%20you)

And don't just think headlights. Your taillights will also be on, making it easier to be seen from behind. Be sure to check your state's laws and the laws of any state within which you'll be traveling, pertaining to the use of headlights.

Driving Side-by-Side on the Interstate

I'm trapped! You'll find drivers who insist on driving right next to you when there's plenty of room to pass you or fall behind.

This is not only dangerous but distracting. You don't need any unnecessary distractions at 70 miles per hour!

In this situation, a car appears to be passing you, but they don't completely pass you. They'll get up next to you, keeping you trapped between them, the car in front of you, and possibly the vehicle to the right of you.

Watch for this and make adjustments to get out of that trap, such as slowing down slightly to create a gap between you and the car in front of you. If the driver next to you doesn't move, try to either drive ahead or slow down. You need to have the option of changing lanes if necessary.

When you're trapped in traffic, your options are limited or none. Make sure you always have an exit plan if something goes wrong. Having a space cushion on all four sides of your car is ideal. Space is a good thing when driving; the more the better!

Stickers/Decals Covering Back Window

Isn't that what the windows are for? It's great to show your loyalty or liking for things by having decals on your car. But please don't cover the windows with them. If you must, place them (sparingly) on the lower corners of the windows, or the car's body.

These decals block the view. There's a reason we have so many windows in a car—to see!

Be careful around those who have decals all over their back windows. They may not be able to see you.

Pedestrians

20 points! ALWAYS be on the lookout for pedestrians. We're mostly focused on looking at the other cars on the road. It's good that you're looking at the cars, but you should be looking out for people on foot, too.

They might be walking with traffic, rather than against traffic, so their back is toward you as you approach them on your side of the road. Maybe nobody ever taught them the right way to walk along a road.

They might be wearing dark colors—which makes them harder to see, especially at night.

Today, many people are walking with earbuds or on their phones. They're often thinking about everything but the cars around them. They will walk across the street without even knowing you're there.

And pedestrians aren't the only ones being distracted by earbuds or phones. Distracted drivers are even less likely to see pedestrians. All the more reason to be focused on your driving, and little else.

When at intersections especially, you should be aware of people on foot and potential moves they might make.

Did you know? In 2019, pedestrians accounted for about 17% of all motor vehicle crash fatalities. Twenty-one percent of pedestrian deaths occurred in hit-and-run accidents. (IIHS, 2021) (Source: https://driving-tests.org/driving-statistics/)

Pay attention to marked pedestrian crossings. Sometimes there are special crosswalks with flashing lights. Many states and towns have laws about stopping for pedestrians. Know them.

Important: Don't wave a pedestrian to pass in front of you if there's a risk another driver might not see them. A car coming up on your left may not see a person to the right of your car.

A pedestrian has no chance against a moving vehicle. Always look out for them.

Driving While Sleepy/Tired

Wake me up when we get . . . to the hospital! If you're feeling tired or sleepy, DO NOT drive. It's so easy to nod off in the blink of an eye—literally. This is serious!

> **Did you know?** Most drivers understand the dangers of drinking and driving and texting and driving, but many people underestimate the dangers of drowsy driving. Each year, drowsy driving accounts for about 100,000 crashes, 71,000 injuries and 1,550 fatalities, according to the National Safety Council (NSC).

Watch for cars that make sudden jerks or swerves. It's likely the driver is either impaired or falling asleep.

Even if you're close to home when you feel your eyelids getting heavy, don't push through—instead, let someone else drive for a while, or, if you're by yourself, pull over at a rest stop for a cup of coffee or two, a walk, something to eat, or even a short nap.

And don't drive when you're sleep-deprived.

Reckless Driving

Grrrrrrr! Some people become race car drivers when they get behind the wheel. It's all fun and games until something goes wrong.

In Florida, reckless driving is defined as:

> "Any person who drives any vehicle in willful or wanton disregard for the safety of persons or property is guilty of reckless driving." (Chapter 316, Section 192, 2022 Florida Statutes)

This is not just about speeding, but overall aggressiveness in everything they do—speeding, passing, weaving, braking, peeling out from a stop, etc.

> **Did you know?** 66% of traffic fatalities are caused by aggressive driving. (SafeMotorist.com, 2019) (Source: https://driving-tests.org/driving-statistics/)

I keep telling you about constantly observing the cars around you, including those coming up behind you, and watching their driving habits. If you see someone driving aggressively, get away from them. Give them plenty of room.

Seat Position

Comfy? You can recline when you get home. You'll see people recline while driving as well as those who look like they're attached to the steering wheel. They're not prepared to handle an emergency.

Sit in an upright position with your arms at around a 100-degree angle. Be comfortable but be in a position to reach and see everything on the dash as well as your mirrors without having to stretch.

Keep a wary eye on drivers who are slouching.

Driving in the Blind Spot

Haha, they can't see me now! Because you're paying attention to the cars coming up behind, you will notice some people get up to your blind spot and then don't move. It's very difficult to see them without turning your head. You need to know they are there.

If you have someone in your blind spot, slow down or speed up to get them out of there. They're a potential accident if you need to change lanes quickly. Always create options. And remember not to drive in someone else's blind spot too.

Driving With Animals

Stay, stay, stay! Most animals love to go for a ride, except to the veterinarian's office! If your pet is too big for a carrier, please make sure Fido is contained to a seat or the floorboard while driving. DO NOT have your pet ride on your lap while driving. Your pet can quickly become distracted, and one sudden move can cause you to lose control of the car.

Also, if you need to reach for something or to turn the wheel on short notice, that pet might be in your way.

Did you know? According to an American Automobile Association (AAA) survey, more than 80 percent of drivers admit that they recognize the dangers of driving with an unrestrained pet, but only 16 percent use pet restraints. (Source: https://www.americanhumane.org/fact-sheet/remember-safety-while-driving-with-pets/)

If your pet rides in the passenger seat, like an unbuckled passenger, they can slide into you if you have to stop or swerve suddenly.

It's not worth the risk. Keep your pets in the back seat unless they're secured. And avoid driving near others if you see a pet running free in the car.

Pulling in Front of You and Slowing

Really? You had to do that? Some drivers will get in front of you from a side road, or another lane, and then take forever to get up to speed. That is, if they don't immediately slow down in front of you to take the next left.

I've mentioned this in other topics—when you enter traffic whether on the interstate, main road, or even a side road, always aim to join in at their rate of speed.

Remember, the actions we take in our car should affect others in the slightest way possible. That's the goal.

Dangerous Passing

Look out! This is something you MUST look for at all times. There are those drivers who will sacrifice their life and everyone else's to gain seven seconds. This may be a car coming toward you or coming up from behind you (an even more dangerous situation).

When someone misjudges the space or opportunity to pass, they most likely will panic and do the wrong thing (like sideswiping you) causing a chain reaction.

This is another reason why keeping a safe distance behind the car in front of you is so important.

On two-lane roads, some people will come right up behind you and tailgate, swerving in and out until they take the chance and pass.

Others will pass you and quickly pull into the lane in front of you, leaving only the slightest space between your car and theirs. And others will take forever to pass.

The bad news is these actions are dangerous and annoying. The good news is they're passing you and will soon be far away from you.

When passing, make your decision far in advance. This allows you time to assess the situation so that when you do pass, it's smooth.

Passing cars on the road is a bit of an art when done correctly:

- Keep a safe distance behind the car to be passed so you have more room to see what's ahead. This is particularly important on two-lane roads.
- Turn on your signal beforehand to allow others to adjust their driving accordingly.
- On a two-lane road, the car behind should slow and the vehicle in front should move slightly to the right, giving the passing car more visibility. This rarely happens but is a nice habit to get into. Anything you can do to make the situation safer is better.
- Ideally, you'll want to turn the steering wheel as little as possible, making it seem as though you're still going straight. This is especially nice for passengers.
- Pass with plenty of space between you and the car in front and don't pull back into the lane in front of the car you passed until you can see that car clearly in your rearview mirror. And then look at least twice to make sure the space is open.

On the interstate, it doesn't take much time for a car two lanes over to fly up and whip into your intended space. If this happens, wait for another chance, and then turn on your signal and move into the next lane when safe.

I like to keep my turn signal on until I'm completely in the lane. The signal lets other drivers know that I'm not there yet.

Now, just because you're in a No Passing Zone and/or there are double solid yellow lines on the road, does not mean some crazy driver isn't going to pass. Do not become complacent in these situations. ALWAYS be on the lookout for the unexpected! Especially with those coming from the opposite direction!

Waiting to Turn Too Far Back

Distance challenged, I guess! This is where you're at a stop sign and want to turn left. Traffic from the left doesn't stop. Someone is waiting to turn toward you from the road to the right, and this driver has the right-of-way.

But instead of pulling up to the point of turning, they sit back a car length or two.

So, when they can turn, they must drive forward and then turn, keeping you from being able to turn left, as you're waiting for them to go first.

This is especially frustrating when there's a lot of traffic and turn opportunities are minimal.

When turning, move to the point where you will make a 90-degree turn. And keep your wheels pointed straight until you turn, so if a car behind hits you, you will go straight and not into oncoming traffic.

Flashing Headlights

Hurry up, hurry up! This is a case of an impatient driver flashing their lights from behind you. Be careful of these aggressive drivers. Do your best to ignore them and move over to let them pass as soon as it's safe.

And I'm sure you'd never do this yourself. It's rude to flash your lights at another driver from behind, and in this current climate of irrational behavior, you're inviting a potentially dangerous confrontation.

Using the Horn

Did you drink too much coffee this morning? The horn is an alarm, not an attitude. People who abuse their horns are often angry and ready for a fight. Don't use your horn to express frustration or anger. Use it only as a warning to avoid a possible accident.

Swerve to Turn

Do you think you're driving a semi? This is a good one. Those who swerve out in the opposite direction of the turn before turning don't have proper perception of space and distance. They turn like they're pulling a 100-foot trailer.

This is dangerous as they could easily bump into an oncoming car on their other side. Their attention is all on their turning destination and they don't even notice the vehicles on their side.

There's no reason why you can't turn from a straight position. Try it, you'll like it!

Follow the Leader

I'd rather not be so attached. I find people who have to drive close behind you, no matter the speed, are more prevalent today because of the use of cell phones. While on the phone, many people will pay the least possible attention to their driving. They will often just focus on the car ahead and drive whatever speed that car is going.

This is especially bothersome on the interstate in the left lane!

If you suspect someone behind you is on the phone, there isn't much you can do other than keep an eye on them.

Emergency Situations

Clear! When you see an emergency vehicle on the side of the road, do your best to slow down and get over, giving them as much room as possible.

This is already a dangerous situation. The people at the emergency site are focused on the emergency, not on you. Don't make it worse by driving too close to the area.

Did you know? The first Move Over law in the United States was passed in South Carolina in 1996, after a paramedic was seriously injured by a passing motor vehicle. By 2012, similar laws were passed in all 50 states with the goal to protect emergency responders working along the roadside, yet one-third of the public is not aware of these laws. (Source: https://www.sheriffs.org/trafficsafety/moveover)

Also, when you hear or see an emergency vehicle ahead of or behind you, try to get over to the right as promptly as you can. These vehicles are trying to reach an emergency as quickly as possible.

Did you know? Because each state has its own legislation, it's important to know the differences in the laws among states if you do a lot of interstate travel. (Source: https://www.motorbiscuit.com/move-over-law-states/)

Too many times drivers will see cars moving to the right and take advantage of this to speed up and pass cars. Move over! Your cooperation may save a life!

Water on the Road

Think ice! Driving on wet roads can be like driving on ice. Especially with tires with worn tread or tires not designed for wet-weather driving.

Don't drive through deep water, as this is likely to cause harm to your car, impair your ability to properly guide the vehicle, and cause a spray that will inhibit your view and the view of others.

If the water is too deep and/or moving, you risk being swept into other vehicles, or even being submerged!

When you're on wet roads, don't use your cruise control. If you do, the car may hydroplane or slide, leaving you with an out-of-control car. You could be headed for a serious accident.

Be aware of driving in the lane near retaining/partition walls when there is water on the road. This area tends to collect more water than the rest of the road (in some cases this excess of water is caused by debris in the drains) and will increase the chances of hydroplaning.

And be considerate of spraying water on pedestrians as you drive by.

Music Too Loud

What did you say? We all like to turn up the volume on our sound system now and then. It's great to rock with the tunes, but overly loud music creates a couple of problems.

First, you get into the music to the point of distraction from driving.

Second, it's irritating to those around you. How have you liked it when, courtesy of another driver near you, you've had to listen to your least-favorite kind of music at high decibels?

Third, and most importantly, with the music loud you will be unable to hear trains, emergency vehicles, and honking (alert honking, in the case of you veering to another lane, off the road, or into an oncoming vehicle).

Earphones/Headphones

Can you hear me now? This is related to playing music too loud, but even worse. With headphones (excuse me, earbuds), you can become immersed in the music (sound) and can be unconscious of the happenings around you.

Did you know? In 2019, distracted driving led to 3,142 fatalities, an estimated 424,000 injuries, and 15% of all police-reported vehicle traffic crashes on US roads. (Source; Virginia Tech Transportation Institute, 2021, https://vtx.vt.edu/articles/2021/10/vtti-national-distracted-driving-coalition.html)

Just sit near a busy street, airport, college, or anywhere young people are walking around. I'll bet most have earbuds in and are oblivious to people and events around them.

Assume those around you—both walking and driving—are wearing earbuds, and drive accordingly.

Shoes

You're not on the beach! Please, don't drive barefoot or in sandals. It only takes a small pebble to get under your foot to make you react, causing you to take your foot off the accelerator, or worse, the brake. Your bare foot doesn't have the solid contact of a shoe. And you're adversely sensitive to the feel of the pedals.

Flip-flops are even worse. They're just the wrong footwear for driving. They can jam, they can come off and get under the pedals, possibly preventing you from stopping, and they can shift on your foot, forcing you to make adjustments while driving.

You can take off your shoes when you get to your destination safely!

Rubbernecking

Whoa, did you see that? While you may not think you're causing any harm by looking at an accident, or at someone pulled over, you'll naturally slow down as you take your mind away from driving and focus on the accident. This slowing will cause those behind you to slow and in a matter of minutes, cars might have to come to a stop a mile behind you.

It's good to slow within reason when passing a distraction like this, but when it occurs on the other side of the road or median, there's no reason to slow at all. Please be conscious of this for the benefit of your fellow drivers.

Even if you don't crash into anything yourself while rubbernecking (and there's a danger of that), you could be the cause of a fender-bender behind you without even knowing it!

Driving With Children

Precious cargo on board! You have three responsibilities when driving with children:

- Get from point A to point B safely.
- Allow other drivers to get from point A to point B safely.
- Get your passengers safely to their destination.

Children should be safely buckled or in an appropriate car seat at all times while in the car. They shouldn't be allowed to roam or move from their seat. Any moving objects (and this most certainly includes people) within the vehicle can cause you to be distracted.

And please, DO NOT leave your children in the car unattended! There are so many reasons. To name a few:

- Heatstroke
- Kidnapping
- The child is not feeling well
- Starting the vehicle if the keys are left in the car (or even worse, the car is running!)
- Leaving the car

Did you know? In 2017–2021, an average of 39 children per year died in overheated vehicles. Since 1998, 805 children have died in overheated vehicles. 88% of them were 3 years of age or younger. 55% of them were one year of age or younger. A young child's body can overheat 3–5 times faster than an adult's body. (KidsandCars.org, 2021) (Source: https://driving-tests.org/driving-statistics/)

Keep the children with you or with another adult. If you see an unattended child, monitor and evaluate the situation and report it if you deem it dangerous. You may be saving the child's life!

Road Rage

Take a chill pill, please! This has become a serious problem. Anger and intolerance have fueled an increase in road rage encounters.

Don't retaliate when someone expresses anger on the road. Avoid the urge to react.

Report any serious road rage incidents immediately. Unfortunately, many of these situations end up deadly.

And as for you, don't instigate any skirmishes while driving. If you've done this in the past, get out of that habit, beginning right now.

Don't let another driver's inconsiderate behavior turn you into a jerk. I understand it can be tempting, but "flipping the bird" when someone makes an ill-advised driving choice can escalate a brief, passing annoyance into a dangerous, even life-threatening situation.

Braking/Riding Brakes

You must like buying new shoes...for your car? Riding the brakes displays a false indication of braking, forcing those behind you to unnecessarily brake or slow down.

This is not only dangerous to those behind you but is also hard on your brakes. Riding the brakes can cause premature wearing of the brakes and may overheat them, reducing their effectiveness.

And let's not forget those who brake (sometimes repeatedly) for no apparent reason. When you see this on the interstate, my guess is these people are overly cautious, timid, afraid, or brand new at driving. Avoid them. You don't know what they're going to do.

Brakes are one of the most important elements of driving. Keep your foot off the brake pedal until you need it.

Driving at Night

I know you're out there! Our reaction time and visibility dramatically lessen at night, especially as we age. Things you see easily during the daylight hours may not appear as quickly at night. Therefore, nighttime driving requires enhanced focus.

If you wear glasses, make sure your prescription is sufficiently up to date, so you have every advantage while night driving. You might need new glasses if other drivers' headlights look like giant yellow blurs!

Be extra alert at night.

Underage Driving

Be patient, your time will come. There's a reason we restrict driving to a minimum age of 16 and require a driver's license. Younger people don't yet have the mental and physical skills to operate a motor vehicle safely.

When you see a very young person driving, give them a wide berth.

And don't allow someone in your family to drive until they're properly prepared and old enough to be licensed. It's not worth the risk to that person and others on the road.

Broken Windshield

Cracked! Do you remember that magazine? It was a humor magazine like *MAD* (1958–2007). Anyway…back to the broken windshield. If you see a car with a damaged windshield, avoid it. The driver's vision is impaired.

If you have a broken windshield, get it fixed immediately.

Not only does a cracked windshield impair your vision, but the windshield can also break apart at any given moment.

In some cases, damage to your windshield and car windows is covered if you have comprehensive insurance. Some states offer glass replacement coverage.

At the time of this writing, three states will waive the deductible for windshield repair. Two of those states waive the entire cost—Kentucky and South Carolina (https://www.carinsurance.com/free-windshield-replacement.aspx).

Driving While Emotional

Why, I oughta…! If you've been in an argument and get in your car mad, you're potentially putting yourself and others at risk. If you're angry your emotions will interfere with your ability to focus on your driving.

> **Did you know?** Driving while crying or visibly angry increased the risk of crashing by 10 times. (Virginia Tech Transportation Institute, 2016) (Source: https://driving-tests.org/driving-statistics/)

Calm down before you get behind the wheel. Driving is a dangerous activity. Driving while angry will only make it more dangerous or, at least, embarrassing. You don't want to lose control racing around a turn and crash into your neighbors' mailboxes, after angrily speeding away from a humdinger argument in your nightclothes.

Be safe, hang onto your self-respect, and live to argue another day.

Parking by the Entrance

I'm only going to be a minute! The road along the front of a store is meant for traffic and deliveries, not parking. By parking there, you're now restricting road space and making it hard for other drivers to see pedestrians coming out from around the front of your car.

If there's enough room for you to park by the entrance without being a giant problem to others, say, if you must park in front of the store to drop off an older person who has trouble walking from the parking lot, at least stay in the car yourself so you can move it out of the way on short notice, if necessary.

There's a reason for parking spaces. Use them! The few seconds you sacrifice by walking from the parking space could prevent an accident, or even save a life.

Seat Belts

Buckle up for safety, buckle up! It's the law. Seat belts save lives. Those who wish to not wear them argue that they should have the freedom to choose. That's all well and good, BUT not wearing a seat belt can affect another person's life, not just your own.

The seat belt can not only save your life and prevent injury in the event of an accident, but will also help you stay firmly in control of the car in situations where you might otherwise be thrown out of control. Losing control of the car may very well result in harm to someone else.

Did you know? A total of 46% of drivers involved in deadly collisions are not buckled up, and a similar number of passengers–47%–were also unbelted in fatal crashes. (Source: Insurance Institute for Highway Safety: Fatality Facts 2020 Yearly Snapshot)

Please keep this in mind the next time you get in the car. The seat belt is not entirely for you, as a driver, but for your passengers too, and for other drivers and their families.

Tinted Windows

Peek-a-boo! I wish there were a ban on tinted windows. Being able to see through all windows of another car helps with our safety.

Each state does have legal limits for the percentage of tint allowed on the different windows of the car. However, it does seem to me that many tints are just too dark.

If a car in front of the car in front of me does something that causes them to swerve, I'd like to know that as far in advance as possible. Being able to see through the windows of the car in front of me would allow me to do so.

Not only do I want to see the driver (to help me determine if they're a focused driver and also to see if they might be signaling me), but I also believe police approaching a car should be able to clearly see the driver's actions.

School Buses

Good morning, children. A lot can be said about driving with school buses on the road. The most basic advice I can offer is to drive as if your child is on that bus.

Be patient around school buses. Their main function is to pick up children on their way to school and drop them off afterward. Because of this, they make frequent stops.

You should only attempt to pass a school bus when in a legal passing zone and do so carefully. School buses have large blind spots making it difficult for the drivers to see smaller vehicles.

And don't ever pass a stopped school bus on the side the children enter and exit.

Maintain a safe distance when driving behind school buses. When driving on roads or highways, drivers should keep at least three car lengths behind any school buses. At highway speeds, this distance should be increased. When a school bus comes to a stop, drivers should stop their vehicles no closer than 10 to 20 feet.

When a school bus is flashing its yellow lights it is preparing to stop, and drivers should prepare to stop their vehicles as well. When the bus is stopped, its red lights are flashing and its stop sign is extended, meaning it's taking on or dropping off passengers. Drivers in either lane are required by law to remain at a stop until the stop sign has been retracted and the flashing red lights are switched off.

Be sure to stop when approaching a school bus from the opposite direction in the opposing lane. This is the law.

Note: You might be surprised to learn that in a handful of states, you must even stop for school buses taking on or letting off passengers on the other side of a divided highway.

Four states—New York, West Virginia, Mississippi, and Arkansas (the latter when the divider is less than 20 feet wide)—require drivers coming the opposite direction to stop on the other side of a divided highway.

Don't learn this the hard way by getting a ticket, being fined, or even temporarily losing your license for getting this wrong in a state with different school bus laws than the ones you're used to. It's well worth looking up the driving laws of states you'll be passing through, as well as knowing your own state's laws. (Source: https://www.drive-safely.net/school-bus-laws/)

Drivers should remember that most school bus-related fatalities occur when drivers attempt to pass a school bus that's at a stop.

Did you know? Most of those schoolchildren who are killed in school bus-related accidents are 5 to 7 years old. They are hit in the "danger zones" around the bus. These are the areas 10 feet in front of the bus, 10 feet behind it, and 10 feet to either side of it. The children are struck either by the school bus itself or by a passing vehicle, even though it is illegal for a vehicle to pass a school bus when its red lights are flashing. (Stanford Children's Health, 2019) (Source: https://driving-tests.org/driving-statistics/)

Even when the red lights and the stop sign have been deactivated, there might still be children in the vicinity. They don't always act in predictable ways and have been known to unexpectedly dart across the road. Drivers should be extra careful when proceeding after a school bus stop.

Please learn the rules of the road and when you must stop for the bus. Err on the side of caution.

Zones

Slow down! Hospital zones and school zones are designated stretches of the road where there's a potential for patients and children to be in or near the road.

I know it's hard to drive 15 miles per hour, especially when you're running late for an appointment, but you'll be even later after you're pulled over for a ticket.

Please obey the speed limits in these zones. It's just the right thing to do.

Handicap Parking

How low can you go? If you don't have the required handicap sticker, license, or registration, DO NOT park in handicap-designated areas! And I don't want to hear that the parking lot was full and you were only going into the store to get one thing.

Also, not all handicaps are visible. Don't judge if someone doesn't look disabled to you. That's none of our business.

If you're not handicapped yourself, in visible or non-visible ways, be thankful.

Driving While Sick

Green around the gills? If you're sick or not feeling well, try to avoid driving. Illness will reduce your ability to function and focus, creating the potential for an accident.

Try to postpone your trip, find someone else to drive you or run errands for you, or (if your ailment isn't contagious) use public transportation.

Parked Cars

Sorry! When you drive by a row of parked cars on your right, you aren't giving much thought to those cars, are you? Well, you should be. A driver's side door of one of those parked cars could swing open at any moment. I've seen it happen many times. Someone in the car isn't paying attention and opens the door into oncoming traffic, causing real damage to both vehicles.

Also, be alert for those who back up first and then look later. Or they're watching traffic or pedestrians in a different direction and fail to see you.

So, while driving through a parking lot or down a street with cars parked to the right, be on the lookout for any movement by a parked car.

Always watch for the reverse lights (Thank goodness for those!).

And it's okay to toot your horn when someone doesn't see you and is about to back into you.

Some helpful advice, courtesy of one driving teacher: whenever possible, park so your next move is forward.

One-Way Street

Wrong way! Just because you see a one-way street sign, don't assume traffic is not coming from the other direction.

Sometimes someone doesn't realize they're going the wrong way. And, believe it or not, some drivers will ignore a one-way street sign. I'm serious, don't be surprised to see someone coming at you from the wrong way!

Also, when watching for oncoming traffic from a one-way street, it's easy to only look at the far lane, as you typically would for a two-way street, forgetting that ALL lanes will be coming your way.

Please, don't be the idiot who takes a shortcut the wrong way through a one-way street. If you do, you might be getting yourself a one-way ticket!

Motorcycles

Watch out for Easy Rider! Motorcycles and bicycles are both vehicles on the road and should obey the same rules as cars and trucks. Not all of them do. There's always the kid on the bike flying in and out of traffic, driving between cars.

Because they can maneuver and accelerate so much quicker than a car or truck, they can sometimes appear out of nowhere.

Some motorcycle riders will position themselves behind you in such a way that they can see ahead of your car. But this also creates the possibility of them being in your blind spot.

Did you know? More than half of all road traffic deaths worldwide are among pedestrians, cyclists, and motorcyclists. (WHO, 2018) (Source: https://driving-tests.org/driving-statistics/)

On a recent trip to California, while creeping along in heavy traffic, we saw motorcycles flying between cars. Motorcycles are allowed to weave in and out of stopped traffic! I just don't get it.

First of all, that's dangerous. And second, why give motorcycles special privileges? Don't get me wrong. I love motorcycles. But I think motorcycles should obey the rules of the road just like cars.

At the time of this writing, California is the only state to allow unrestricted lane splitting.

Four other states allow a modified law, basically saying "when safe to do so." Twelve states have no law on the books concerning lane splitting.

Please keep a lookout for motorcycles. They're not as easy to see as cars, and we're just not expecting to see them. All I can say is always be aware of what's coming up behind you.

Yield

Wait, wait...at least slow down! Yield to oncoming traffic with the right-of-way. Simple, right? Apparently, not so much. I've seen people race through a yield sign to get ahead rather than slowing down and waiting for a car to pass by.

> **Did you know?** The National Safety Council estimates that roughly 15% of all automobile accidents are caused when motorists fail to yield to traffic on the road. (Source: National Safety Council)

Yes, the yield sign is not a stop sign, but it should be treated as one. When approaching a yield sign, apply the same habits as approaching a stop sign. However, you only need to stop if you risk hitting right-of-way traffic.

Railroad Crossings

Stop, look, and listen!! Railroad crossings pose a serious risk for accidents. Many people drive right up to the line or gate. This is too close! And some even try to beat the train. They think it's a thrilling rush, but the consequences of an accident with a train have been grave for many.

When approaching a railroad crossing, slow down and look in both directions. Be sure to test your brakes in advance. You should also lower your windows and turn off the radio or earbuds. Don't get on the phone. Listen for the train's warning whistles. Try to stop no closer than 15 feet and no farther than 50 feet from the tracks.

Once the train has passed, wait. There may be another train coming from the opposite direction.

Trailers (Campers)

Beware of trailers! Being able to successfully maneuver a trailer takes a lot of experience. And experience comes from what? That's right, failure. When a trailer comes loose, chaos and usually lots of damage follow.

Trailers come in all sizes, shapes, and mechanical conditions. It's not uncommon for someone to forget to do something when hooking up the trailer.

When coming up to or behind a trailer, look it over carefully, and determine its safeness. If the trailer is beaten up and the lights on the trailer aren't working, odds are the driver is careless.

Watch out for a weaving trailer, as its driver can lose control in an instant.

Earlier in the book, I mention trailers in "Attachments to the Vehicle." Not only do you want to watch the trailer and the vehicle towing it, but also any items on or in the trailer.

Backing Up on the Exit

Whoops! When you're approaching an exit, look out for those who realize, after getting on the exit ramp, they've taken the wrong exit—and are backing up to reenter the highway!

Please resist the impulse to do this. People have been killed by drivers making this numb-skull move. Just go ahead and make the exit. It will only take a few minutes to find your way back onto the highway again. You can do it.

Semis/Tractor Trailers

Show some respect! It's difficult enough for professional truck drivers to deal with all the passenger cars on the road. The road is their office and we should respect their space.

When you see a semi ahead, pay attention and give it space. They often get trapped in car traffic and may want to make a move to get clear.

Visibility around a semi is difficult at best when driving too close behind. Stay back when following a semi through a traffic light. If you are too close, you may not see that the light has changed before you enter the intersection.

Did you know? According to the National Highway Traffic Safety Administration (NHTSA), tire blowouts account for more than 12,000 truck accidents annually, many of them causing injuries and fatalities, not to mention property damage. (Source: https://wilshirelawfirm.com/blog/personal-injury-law/truck-tire-blowouts/)

Be aware that the tires on the trucks can come apart at any time. You've probably seen evidence of this along highways, big strips of tire that have peeled off.

These tires, or parts of tires, become projectiles and can cause severe damage upon impact. Stay vigilant when coming up to a semi.

Because of their size, semis create turbulence caused by the air flowing around the trailer. This turbulence can cause an adjacent car, or one behind the semi, to lose control. Be cautious. Keep your distance, and also be aware of other cars that seem too close to the semi.

One more thing. If you are approaching the side of a tractor trailer at a turn, be aware that the driver may cut off your lane when turning. Stay back to provide ample space for their turn. You can easily get crunched if you are too close.

One More Thing...

If you do get pulled over by the police, I suggest you do the following:

- Slow down and pull over at the first safe opportunity.
- Turn off the ignition.
- Roll down your window.
- Place both hands on the steering so the officer can clearly see them.
- Be polite.
- Always have your license, registration, and insurance card in a close and convenient location.
- Do as the officer says.
- Let the officer know if you have a weapon in the car.
- When the traffic stop is complete, and the officer has safely returned to their vehicle, proceed to enter the highway in a safe and responsible manner.

Thank you!

Afterword

I hope you enjoyed riding along with me and learning about the many bad driving habits that I believe are the cause of most accidents.

Hopefully, after reading this book, you understand what bad and dangerous driving is, how to avoid it, and what you should do to be a good and safe driver.

As I mentioned previously, (and I mention it again because it's very important!) in addition to learning these habits, please study all the rules of the road for your state and other states through which you will be driving. Driving laws are not the same in all states.

And, before you even start the car, here (in no particular order) is a checklist of basic things to do before driving:

- Walk around the vehicle and check the car's overall condition.
- See that your car is mechanically sound and everything is working correctly.
- Adjust your seat.
- Set your mirrors.
- Adjust your headrest.
- Adjust the steering wheel.

- Secure any loose items.
- Make sure driver and passengers are buckled up.
- Keep your car registration and insurance current. Have both certificates in the vehicle and readily available.
- See that all lights are working correctly.
- Check your windshield wiper fluid and ensure your wipers and blades work well.
- Make sure you have plenty of fuel and/or battery charge to get to your destination.
- Check your dashboard for any warning lights.
- Make sure all windows are clean.
- Remove anything that blocks your view of the road.
- Adjust the seat so you can reach all controls.
- Lock the doors.
- Read this book again!

I hope you have enjoyed this book and I look forward to seeing you on the road.

And thank you for not . . .

Driving Me Crazy!

About the Author

John Reinhardt has been designing books for 48 years with nearly 3,000 books to his credit. This is his first book as an author.

John lives in a golf community in central Florida with his wife, Lynn. When he is not designing books or writing, he spends his time playing golf, gardening, brewing, target shooting, creating things, playing guitar, shooting pool, and just about anything else there is to do.

Most of all, John enjoys driving. He is a Formula 1 and IndyCar fan. Four of his favorite cars were two Porsche 911s ('72 and '76), a '73 BMW Bavaria, and a 2009 Mini Cooper S. Occasionally, John will race go-karts at nearby tracks. He has yet to beat his daughter in a race.

You can contact John at:
john@bookdesign.com

For updates and information:

www.youredrivingmecrazy.com

Printed in Great Britain
by Amazon